NORTH AMERICAN
FIELD GUIDES

SNAKES

Angela Lim

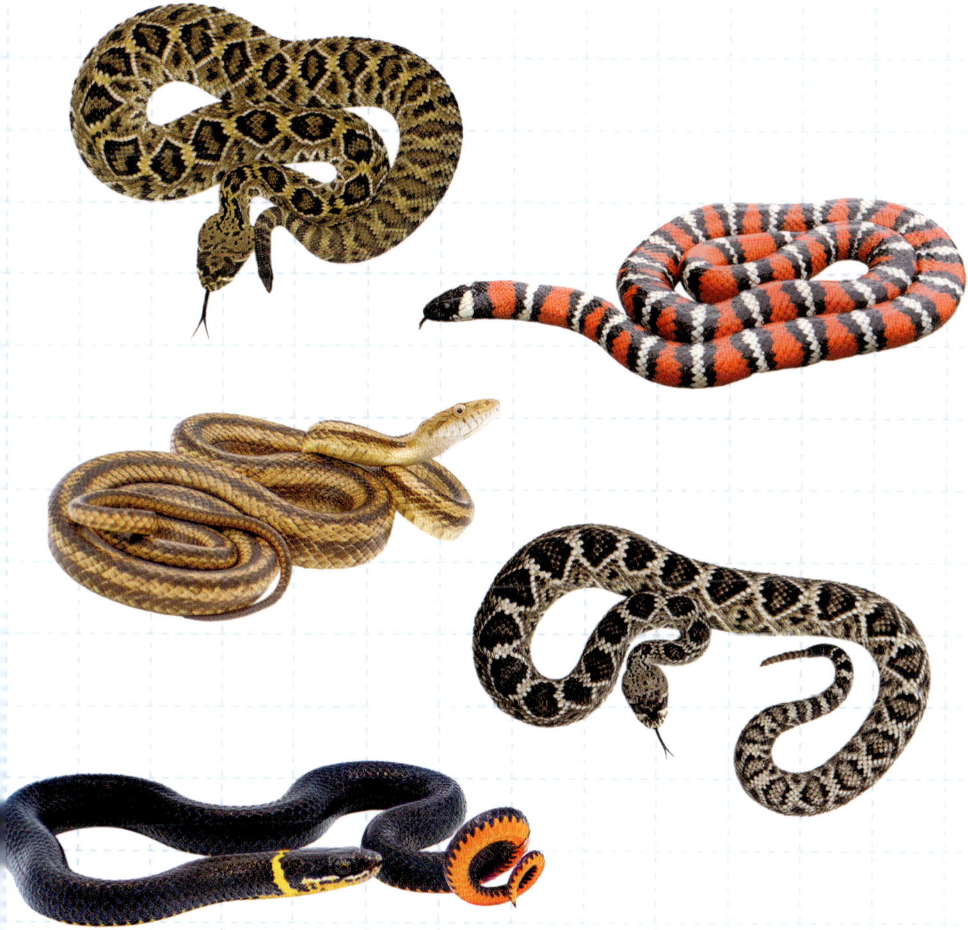

An Imprint of Abdo Reference | abdobooks.com

CONTENTS

Elapids

Vipers

WHAT ARE SNAKES?

Snakes are scaly, limbless reptiles that hunt other animals such as birds, small mammals, fish, and insects. Most snakes have flexible jaws and swallow their prey whole. They have forked tongues that they use to bring odors to a smelling organ inside their mouths. Snakes do not have eyelids or ear flaps.

SNAKE CATEGORIES

There are about 150 snake species native to North America. These snakes are categorized into two main groups: venomous and nonvenomous. Venomous snakes use a toxic substance called venom mixed with saliva to hunt. Less than 10 percent of snake species in North America are venomous. Nonvenomous snakes may have small amounts of toxins in their saliva. But they do not have enough venom to harm people.

Venomous and nonvenomous snakes can be divided into smaller groups, such as families. Snakes in the same family share certain features and behaviors. Each North American snake species belongs to one of five families:

- Blind snakes: Blind snakes are nonvenomous and have small eyes. They spend most of their lives underground.
- Boas: Boas are nonvenomous snakes that kill by constriction.
- Colubrids: More than two-thirds of snake species belong to the Colubridae family. Colubrids have large scales on their bellies and few scales on their heads. Most colubrids are nonvenomous.
- Elapids: Elapids are fast-moving venomous snakes.

- Vipers: Vipers are the most common group of venomous snakes in North America. Some vipers have pit organs on their heads that detect heat. This feature helps them hunt.

SNAKE IDENTIFICATION

Snakes are usually solitary and can be hard to find. Some signs can indicate if a snake is nearby. Snakes regularly shed their skins. Finding a snakeskin can be a sign that a snake is in the area. People can also check the ground for slither marks.

After finding a snake, certain characteristics can help with identification. In addition to color and pattern, the shape and size of a snake's head, tail, and eyes can help people figure out the species. Scale texture varies between species, making a snake look smooth or rough. Behavior and location also provide helpful clues to snake identification.

HOW TO USE THIS BOOK

Tab shows the snake category.

COLUBRIDS

DIAMOND-BACKED WATER SNAKE *(NERODIA RHOMBIFER)*

The snake's common name appears here.

…backed water snakes are large snakes with thick … scales. The… pattern … snakes liv… fish. They … Diamond-… and bring them … have a reputation for being aggres… only if needed. They flee into the w… snakes also defend themselves by r… foul-smelling musk.

Fun Facts give interesting information about snakes.

FUN FACT
Diamond-backed water snakes can stay underwater for about one hour before they need to come up for air.

How to Spot boxes give information about the snake's size, range, habitat, and diet.

HOW TO SPOT

Length: 2.5 to 4 feet (0.8 to 1.2 m)
North American Range: Mississippi River Valley, southern United States, and northern Mexico
Habitat: Swamps and marshes
Diet: Freshwater fish and frogs

24

EASTERN HOGNOSE S

(HETERODON PLATIRHINOS)

The snake's scientific name appears here.

The eastern hognose snake has a heavy body, wide head, and upturned nose. Its coloration can vary widely. It may appear yellow or brown, but individuals can also be orange, gray, or slightly red. Some have a pattern of dark splotches on the back, but they can also be a solid color. The eastern hognose snake is nonaggressive and has a range of defensive techniques. It inflates its neck and hisses loudly. It also plays dead. The snake rolls onto its back and thrashes wildly before falling still. It releases a foul-smelling odor. It plays dead for several minutes before fleeing to

This paragraph gives information about the snake.

HOW

Length 2.8 feet (

North American Range: Southern Canada and eastern

...ed

...ıds

...er amphibians, small mammals, and invertebrates

Images show the snake.

Playing dead

POPPING TOADS

Toads make up most of the eastern hognose snake's diet. These amphibians can inflate themselves in defense. The snake has sharp fangs at the back of its jaw. These fangs puncture the toad and cause it to deflate, making the prey easier to swallow.

25

Sidebars provide additional information about the topic.

TEXAS BLIND SNAKE *(RENA DULCIS)*

Texas blind snakes spend most of their time underground. With their pinkish-brown scales, these snakes are often mistaken for earthworms. Texas blind snakes have small eyes that look like black dots. While these snakes have poor vision, they are not completely blind. Their eyes can detect changes in light. Texas blind snakes eat mostly the larvae of ants and termites. Ants and termites usually attack invaders, but Texas blind snakes secrete smelly chemicals that discourage the insects.

HOW TO SPOT

Length: 4 to 12 inches (10 to 30 cm)

North American Range: Southwestern United States, northern Mexico

Habitat: Underground in prairies and deserts

Diet: Larvae of ants and termites

AN UNLIKELY RELATIONSHIP

Screech owls have a unique relationship with Texas blind snakes. An owl carries one of these snakes to its nest. Unlike with most prey, the owl brings the snake to the nest alive. The snake eats parasites there, increasing the chance of survival for the young owls.

WESTERN BLIND SNAKE

(RENA HUMILIS)

Western blind snakes are small snakes with rounded heads and tails. They look similar to earthworms, but their scales give them a shinier appearance. These snakes range in color, appearing pale brown, pink, or slightly purple. Western blind snakes spend most of their lives underground. They do not have a strong sense of vision. Their small, round eyes can detect only light. The snakes depend on their sense of smell to hunt. They can detect ant pheromones. They follow these scent trails to ant nests.

HOW TO SPOT

Length: Up to 1.3 feet (0.4 m)

North American Range: Southern California to Texas, north-central Mexico

Habitat: Underground in mountain brush and desert grasslands

Diet: Ants, termites, insect eggs, and larvae

Female with eggs

ROSY BOA *(LICHANURA TRIVIRGATA)*

The rosy boa is named for the color of its belly. The rest of its body is mostly bluish gray. It has three stripes that run along the length of its body. These stripes can be black, brown, or reddish orange. Rosy boas often hide under rocks and logs. They ambush their prey, which consists mostly of small mammals. Rosy boas hold on to their prey with their strong jaws. Like all boas, these snakes kill by constriction. Rosy boas also hide for protection from predators. If spotted by a predator, the boa coils into a ball. The snake pretends its tail is its head. It waves its tail to make it look like a snake head about to strike.

HOW TO SPOT

Length: 1.4 to 3.7 feet (0.4 to 1.1 m)

North American Range: Southwestern United States into Mexico

Habitat: Deserts and rocky shrublands

Diet: Wood rats and small mammals

FUN FACT

Most snakes lay eggs. But rosy boas give birth to live young.

RUBBER BOA *(CHARINA BOTTAE)*

Rubber boas are solitary creatures. They are nocturnal but occasionally sun themselves during the day. Rubber boas have dark backs that may be brown, tan, or olive. Their bellies are a lighter color, such as yellow or cream. The snakes' two-toned appearance is similar to another snake species, the western yellow-bellied racer. The two species differ in behavior. Rubber boas move slowly and are not aggressive. Even when threatened, rubber boas rarely attack creatures that are not their prey. A rubber boa tricks predators into attacking the snake's tail. It also releases a strong odor to deter predators.

HOW TO SPOT

Length: 1.2 to 2.8 feet (0.4 to 0.9 m)

North American Range: British Columbia, Canada, and northwestern United States

Habitat: Prairies, shrublands, grasslands, and forests

Diet: Small mammals, birds, and amphibians

BLACK SWAMP SNAKE

(SEMINATRIX PYGAEA)

Black swamp snakes are a shiny black color. They have red or reddish-orange bellies. Female snakes of this species outweigh males. They have longer bodies, while males have thicker tails. Black swamp snakes spend much of their lives in or near water. Because they live in aquatic habitats, these snakes are sensitive to droughts. They enter a state of estivation during these extended periods of hot, dry weather. Estivation is similar to hibernation, except it occurs during the summer. It is a period of inactivity when an animal survives by using very little energy.

HOW TO SPOT

Length: 10 to 15 inches (25 to 38 cm)

North American Range: Southeastern United States

Habitat: Aquatic habitats, especially bays and bogs

Diet: Aquatic creatures, especially salamanders and leeches

BLACKNECK GARTER SNAKE

(THAMNOPHIS CYRTOPSIS)

Blackneck garter snakes are named for two black patches of scales on their necks. Their overall color ranges from dark gray to olive gray. A thick stripe runs from the base of the head to the tip of the tail. The stripe appears yellow or orange close to the head and becomes whiter as it runs along the body. Thinner white stripes run along both sides of the body. Blackneck garter snakes are often found near water. They are most active during the day. When threatened, they flatten their heads. This makes them appear larger to scare off predators.

HOW TO SPOT

Length: 1.3 to 2.3 feet (0.4 to 0.7 m)

North American Range: Southwestern United States to Mexico

Habitat: Near forest and scrubland streams and ponds

Diet: Frogs, toads, and tadpoles

FUN FACT

Blackneck garter snakes communicate mainly through scent. They release scents called pheromones to communicate with each other.

BROWN WATER SNAKE

(NERODIA TAXISPILOTA)

Brown water snakes are brown with dark brown splotches along their bodies. These snakes are semiaquatic. They are often found near fresh water. They sun themselves on branches and dive in the water to hunt. Their eyes and nostrils are located near the tops of their heads, which allows them to see and breathe when swimming. Brown water snakes prey mainly on catfish. They eat animals such as lizards and frogs when catfish are scarce. Catfish have sharp spines in their fins. Scientists have seen these spines sticking out from brown water snakes. But they do not appear to cause long-term harm to the snakes. These large snakes are nonvenomous. However, they may bite when threatened.

HOW TO SPOT

Length: 1.7 to 5.8 feet (0.5 to 1.8 m)

North American Range: Southeastern United States

Habitat: Near rivers and large streams

Diet: Small catfish

BUTLER'S GARTER SNAKE

(THAMNOPHIS BUTLERI)

Butler's garter snakes are dark brown. They have three stripes that run down their bodies. The stripes may be yellow, orange, or cream. The Butler's garter snake has a narrow head compared to other garter snake species. These snakes are solitary creatures. But they sometimes gather in groups to hibernate in underground burrows during the winter. Like many snake species, Butler's garter snakes have a strong sense of smell. They smell using their tongues. They also are sensitive to vibrations, which help them detect movement. These snakes release a strong odor when threatened. They also thrash wildly to startle predators and escape.

HOW TO SPOT

Length: 1.3 to 2.4 feet (0.4 to 0.7 m)
North American Range: Great Lakes region
Habitat: Wetlands
Diet: Earthworms, leeches, small frogs, and salamanders

CALIFORNIA MOUNTAIN KINGSNAKE *(LAMPROPELTIS ZONATA)*

California mountain kingsnakes are colorful snakes with red, yellowish-white, and black bands. The top of the head is black, while the chin and throat are usually white. The first band at the base of the head is white. California mountain kingsnakes are usually most active during the day. Kingsnakes spend much of their time on the ground but are also known to climb trees. Males sense pheromones from female snakes when it is time to mate. Females lay eggs that hatch after about 60 days.

HOW TO SPOT

Length: 1.6 to 4.2 feet (0.5 to 1.3 m)

North American Range: Parts of Washington and Oregon, California, and Mexico

Habitat: Forests

Diet: Lizards, birds, eggs, and other snakes

FRIEND OR FOE?

Coral snakes and kingsnakes look very similar. Both have yellowish, black, and red bands along their bodies. Being able to tell the difference is important. Coral snakes are venomous. Kingsnakes are not. The order of the bands differs. Coral snakes have yellow and red bands that touch each other. If black bands separate the yellowish-white and red bands, the snake is a kingsnake.

CAT-EYED SNAKE

(LEPTODEIRA SEPTENTRIONALIS)

Cat-eyed snakes live in a variety of habitats. They are found in semiarid deserts and rainforests from southern Texas into parts of South America. These snakes have large, yellowish eyes with vertical pupils, similar to a cat's pupils. The snake's head is wider than its neck. Cat-eyed snakes tend to be light brown to pale orange. They have saddle-shaped dark splotches along their long bodies. Cat-eyed snakes do not climb trees, but their slender bodies allow them to peer into low-hanging branches to locate prey.

FUN FACT

Cat-eyed snakes have fangs at the rear of the mouth. The fangs inject weak venom that is harmless to humans.

HOW TO SPOT

Length: 8.9 to 39 inches (23 to 98 cm)

North American Range: Texas, Mexico, and Central America

Habitat: Scrublands and rainforests

Diet: Frogs and other amphibians, lizards, small fish, and mice

CHECKERED GARTER SNAKE

(THAMNOPHIS MARCIANUS)

The checkered garter snake has a checkerboard pattern of black marks covering its body. The rest of the snake is usually green or gray in color. The snake has several other markings in addition to its checkerboard pattern. A cream crescent patch lies on either side of the head. The snake also has pale yellow stripes running down its back and sides. The checkered garter snake is a strong swimmer. It hunts for prey in rivers. It also flees into the water to hide from predators.

HOW TO SPOT

Length: 1.5 to 3.5 feet (0.5 to 1.1 m)

North American Range: Southwestern United States, Mexico, and Central America

Habitat: Near water in deserts, savannas, and grasslands

Diet: Earthworms, mice, fish, lizards, slugs, amphibians, and eggs

COACHWHIP *(MASTICOPHIS FLAGELLUM)*

Coachwhips are found throughout much of the United States and Mexico. They live from coast to coast and as far north as Kansas. Coachwhips are large snakes. They can grow to more than eight feet (2.4 m) long. Their color varies from black to brown to red. The tail is often lighter than the head. Coachwhips are named for their long tails, which resemble a braided whip. Their large eyes help them hunt. They are fast-moving predators that chase prey. They can be aggressive and even pursue people if startled. Coachwhips may ambush their prey, especially during hot weather when they can lie in wait in the shade.

HOW TO SPOT

Length: 3 to 8 feet (0.9 to 2.4 m) or longer

North American Range: United States and Mexico

Habitat: Shrublands, grasslands, and savannas

Diet: Lizards and other reptiles, small mammals, amphibians, insects, and carrion

COMMON GARTER SNAKE

(THAMNOPHIS SIRTALIS)

The common garter snake is one of the most widespread snakes in North America. It is common in most regions except the US Southwest, where the climate is dry. The 13 subspecies are grouped by region. The snake's appearance varies across these subspecies. The common garter snake may be black, brown, gray, or green. Some snakes have red spots. Most subspecies have three brightly colored stripes along the length of their bodies. These stripes are usually yellow but can also be white, green, or brown. Some common garter snakes can be entirely black.

HOW TO SPOT

Length: 1.5 to 4.5 feet (0.5 to 1.4 m)

North American Range: Canada, United States, and northern Mexico

Habitat: Grasslands, especially near water

Diet: Earthworms, amphibians, leeches, slugs, snails, crayfish, small fish, and other snakes

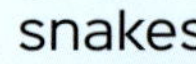

AN EVOLUTIONARY RACE

Common garter snakes prey on rough-skinned newts. These amphibians produce a toxin that is deadly to most predators. But common garter snakes have evolved to become resistant to the toxin. As a result, the newts have evolved to produce even stronger toxin to protect themselves from the snakes. The cycle continues.

COMMON KINGSNAKE

(LAMPROPELTIS GETULA)

Common kingsnakes have shiny black bodies covered with a white or yellow chain-like pattern. These large snakes can grow up to seven feet (2.1 m) long. Common kingsnakes live in a variety of habitats, including urban and suburban areas. These snakes are important in their ecosystems. They eat a variety of animals, including rattlesnakes and other venomous snakes. They help limit the population of snakes that are dangerous to people. Common kingsnakes use constriction to kill their prey.

FUN FACT
Common kingsnakes are immune to viper venom.

HOW TO SPOT

Length: 3 to 7 feet (0.9 to 2.1 m)

North American Range: United States and Mexico

Habitat: Forests, fields, shrublands, urban areas, and wetland areas

Diet: Small mammals, amphibians, birds, bird eggs, lizards, and other snakes

CORN SNAKE *(PANTHEROPHIS GUTTATUS)*

The corn snake is reddish orange. Dark red spots cover its body. Its striking appearance makes it a popular pet. Different colors and patterns are possible through breeding. Corn snakes are most active during the day. They climb trees to hunt prey. These snakes are generally nonaggressive. They flee for shelter or freeze in place if they feel threatened. If escape is not possible, they may vibrate their tails rapidly to create a buzzing sound. They bite only if needed.

HOW TO SPOT

Length: 2.5 to 4 feet (0.8 to 1.2 m)

North American Range: Eastern United States

Habitat: Woodlands and swamps

Diet: Lizards, frogs, rodents, birds, and bird eggs

DEKAY'S BROWN SNAKE

(STORERIA DEKAYI)

Dekay's brown snake is brown or gray in color. It has a brown stripe down its back. Two rows of small, brown spots lie on either side of this stripe. The top of the snake's head is dark. Dekay's brown snake also has a dark spot underneath each eye. The snake spends most of its time underground. It comes to the surface during periods of heavy rain. It tends to be active at night. Dekay's brown snake has long teeth that grasp prey. It then swallows the live prey. Females give birth to live young in late summer to early fall.

HOW TO SPOT

Length: 9 to 20 inches (23 to 51 cm)

North American Range: Southern Canada, United States, and northern Mexico

Habitat: Moist forests, grasslands, and wetland areas

Diet: Slugs, earthworms, snails, and insects

DIAMOND-BACKED WATER SNAKE *(NERODIA RHOMBIFER)*

Diamond-backed water snakes are large snakes with thick bodies. They have rough scales. They can be gray or light brown in color. A chain-like pattern of darker splotches covers their backs. These snakes live near water and hunt aquatic animals, such as fish. They capture prey in their jaws and bring them to shore. Diamond-backed water snakes have a reputation for being aggressive. However, they bite only if needed. They flee into the water if threatened. The snakes also defend themselves by releasing a foul-smelling musk.

FUN FACT

Diamond-backed water snakes can stay underwater for about one hour before they need to come up for air.

HOW TO SPOT

Length: 2.5 to 4 feet (0.8 to 1.2 m)

North American Range: Mississippi River Valley, southern United States, and northern Mexico

Habitat: Swamps and marshes

Diet: Freshwater fish and frogs

EASTERN HOGNOSE SNAKE

(HETERODON PLATIRHINOS)

The eastern hognose snake has a heavy body, wide head, and upturned nose. Its coloration can vary widely. It may appear yellow or brown, but individuals can also be orange, gray, or slightly red. Some have a pattern of dark splotches on the back, but they can also be a solid color. The eastern hognose snake is nonaggressive and has a range of defensive techniques. It inflates its neck and hisses loudly. It also plays dead. The snake rolls onto its back and thrashes wildly before falling still. It releases a foul-smelling odor. It plays dead for several minutes before fleeing to safety.

HOW TO SPOT

Length: 1.7 to 2.8 feet (0.5 to 0.9 m)

North American Range: Southern Canada and eastern and central United States

Habitat: Woodlands and forest edges

Diet: Toads, other amphibians, small mammals, and invertebrates

Playing dead

POPPING TOADS

Toads make up most of the eastern hognose snake's diet. These amphibians can inflate themselves in defense. The snake has sharp fangs at the back of its jaw. These fangs puncture the toad and cause it to deflate, making the prey easier to swallow.

EASTERN INDIGO SNAKE

(DRYMARCHON COUPERI)

The eastern indigo snake is a glossy black color. It has a purple sheen when viewed in the sunlight. Its belly is lighter in color. The snake's chin may be red, orange, or black. The eastern indigo snake is nonvenomous and nonaggressive. It vibrates its tail and hisses loudly when threatened. Habitat destruction is a major threat to this snake. It often shelters in gopher burrows, which are disturbed during land development.

HOW TO SPOT

Length: 5 to 6.8 feet (1.5 to 2.1 m)

North American Range: Southeastern United States

Habitat: Scrublands, woodlands, prairies, and marshy areas

Diet: Mammals, frogs, lizards, fish, eggs, birds, and other snakes

EASTERN RACER

(COLUBER CONSTRICTOR)

Eastern racers have a shiny appearance because of their smooth scales. They have black bodies and whitish chins and throats. They are long, slender snakes that tend to flee from danger. If escape is not possible, they vibrate their tails as a warning. They strike and bite only if needed. Eastern racers are opportunistic feeders. This means they eat whatever prey is available to them. These snakes cover a wide range in the United States. They can live in a variety of habitats. Their diets vary depending on the habitat and region.

FUN FACT

Despite its name, the racer moves at only about four miles per hour (6.4 kmh).

HOW TO SPOT

Length: 1.7 to 4.7 feet (0.5 to 1.4 m)

North American Range: Eastern United States

Habitat: Woodlands and prairies

Diet: Small mammals, birds, eggs, reptiles, amphibians, insects, and spiders

EASTERN RAT SNAKE

(PANTHEROPHIS ALLEGHANIENSIS)

The eastern rat snake is a large, glossy snake with many color variants. It may be black, yellow, orange, tan, or gray. Its belly is a lighter color than its back. White scales mark its throat and chin. The snake is a strong swimmer and climber. It can climb steep cliffs. The snake also climbs trees in search of bird eggs. The eastern rat snake is slow moving and nonaggressive. It does not have a rattle but shakes its tail when threatened. It bites only if needed.

FUN FACT

The different color variants of the eastern rat snake were once thought to be different species. But genetic testing showed that the DNA among the color variants was extremely similar.

HOW TO SPOT

Length: 3.5 to 7 feet (1.1 to 2.1 m)

North American Range: Eastern United States

Habitat: Fields and woodlands

Diet: Lizards, frogs, birds, and bird eggs

EASTERN RIBBON SNAKE

(THAMNOPHIS SAURITA)

The eastern ribbon snake is a thin, dark snake with rough scales. It has three light-colored stripes on its body. The eastern ribbon snake moves quickly. It chases prey such as frogs. It also uses its speed to flee from predators, including herons and raccoons. It is a strong swimmer and often escapes into water. Eastern ribbon snakes are diurnal, active during the day. They tend to be solitary but are sometimes spotted in groups.

HOW TO SPOT

Length: 1.5 to 2.2 feet (0.5 to 0.7 m)

North American Range: Southern Canada and eastern United States

Habitat: Wet woodlands, prairies, marshes, and bogs

Diet: Frogs, salamanders, and small fish

FLAT-HEADED SNAKE

(TANTILLA GRACILIS)

The flat-headed snake is a small snake. It is gray or light brown. Its head is slightly darker than the rest of its body. The snake has a salmon-pink belly. This color differentiates it from other small burrowing snakes. The flat-headed snake spends much of its time underground in moist soil. It occasionally emerges during late spring or early summer to mate. Females lay their eggs in underground burrows and crevices, or narrow openings, in rock. Multiple females may all lay eggs in the same spot.

HOW TO SPOT

Length: 7 to 8 inches (18 to 20 cm)
North American Range: Missouri, Kansas, and Texas and along the Mississippi River
Habitat: Open, rocky hillsides
Diet: Scorpions, spiders, centipedes, insects, and larvae

FLORIDA CROWNED SNAKE

(TANTILLA RELICTA)

The Florida crowned snake is a small, thin snake with smooth scales. It has a tan body and a dark head and neck. A pale band of scales separates the head from the neck. A pale splotch lies near the back of the eyes. The Florida crowned snake is nocturnal and rarely comes to the surface. It spends much of its life underground, where it preys on beetle larvae. The snake often hides under rocks, rotting logs, and leaf litter. It is also known to use the burrows of other animals such as gophers and tortoises. The Florida crowned snake wriggles wildly to avoid capture. It also releases a foul odor to protect itself.

HOW TO SPOT

Length: 7 to 9 inches (18 to 23 cm)
North American Range: Florida and a few places in southern Georgia
Habitat: Sandhills and woodlands
Diet: Beetle larvae, centipedes, and snails

GIANT GARTER SNAKE

(THAMNOPHIS GIGAS)

The giant garter snake is one of the largest garter snake species. It is olive or brown with an orange stripe running down its back. It also has a lighter stripe on each side of its body. The giant garter snake depends on wetland habitats to survive. Its diet includes aquatic prey such as fish and tadpoles. It spends the winter in underground burrows near its hunting grounds. Habitat destruction is a major threat to giant garter snakes. The snake has adapted to survive near canals and rice fields. But only about 5 percent of its original wetland habitat remains.

HOW TO SPOT

Length: 3 to 5.4 feet (0.9 to 1.6 m)

North American Range: Central California

Habitat: Wetlands and other places near fresh water

Diet: Small fish, frogs, and tadpoles

GLOSSY CRAYFISH SNAKE

(LIODYTES RIGIDA)

Glossy crayfish snakes have shiny olive or brown bodies. Their bellies are yellow with dark crescent markings. They have rough scales, yellow lips, and large eyes. Glossy crayfish snakes are named after their favorite prey. The snakes have chisel-like teeth that help them grip crayfish shells. Glossy crayfish snakes spend most of their lives in water. They occasionally bask in nearby trees. They are nocturnal and hunt at night. People rarely encounter them. Glossy crayfish snakes may dive to the bottom of a body of water to escape predators.

HOW TO SPOT

Length: 1.2 to 2 feet (0.4 to 0.6 m)
North American Range: Southeastern United States
Habitat: Canals, swamps, and other wetlands
Diet: Crayfish, small fish, salamanders, frogs, dragonfly larvae, and beetles

GLOSSY SNAKE *(ARIZONA ELEGANS)*

The glossy snake has a shiny appearance. It is beige or gray with a pattern of dark patches covering its body. The patches may be gold, brown, or olive gray and are rimmed with black scales. The glossy snake is nocturnal. During the day, it hides under rocks or burrows underground. Its lower jaw fits into the upper jaw to prevent sand from entering its mouth when burrowing. It also has small eyes because it spends much of its time underground. Female glossy snakes lay eggs every other year. The eggs hatch between August and September. Female glossy snakes protect their offspring for a few days after hatching.

HOW TO SPOT

Length: 2.5 to 5.9 feet (0.8 to 1.8 m)

North American Range: Southwestern United States and Mexico

Habitat: Prairies and deserts

Diet: Lizards and small mammals

GOPHER SNAKE *(PITUOPHIS CATENIFER)*

Gopher snakes are large snakes. Their coloration varies across their range and tends to match surrounding vegetation. They may be light yellow or gray. Brown or black patches cover the back. The belly is white with black spots. A small black stripe runs from the corners of the jaw and over the snout. Gopher snakes have distinct tails marked with black bands. They mimic rattlesnakes and shake their tails when threatened. However, gopher snakes lack the true rattle of rattlesnakes. Gopher snakes are defensive and bite when threatened. Their other defensive actions include hissing and coiling. They also puff their bodies and flatten their heads to appear bigger.

HOW TO SPOT

Length: 5.9 to 9 feet (1.8 to 2.7 m)

North American Range: Southwestern Canada and western and central United States

Habitat: Woodlands, deserts, and grasslands

Diet: Small mammals, birds, lizards, insects, eggs, and other snakes

GRAHAM'S CRAYFISH SNAKE

(REGINA GRAHAMII)

Graham's crayfish snake is a dull brown color. It has a yellow or tan stripe on its side. Its underside is yellow or cream. Freshly molted crayfish make up most of its diet. These crayfish are easier to digest than those with hard shells. Graham's crayfish snake also shelters and hibernates in crayfish burrows. The snake is common in its range. It often basks on tree branches during the spring and summer. It is active mainly during the day, but it shifts to nocturnal behavior during the hottest parts of summer.

HOW TO SPOT

Length: 1.5 to 2.3 feet (0.5 to 0.7 m)

North American Range: Central United States

Habitat: Near lakes, ponds, and slow-moving water

Diet: Primarily freshly molted crayfish, amphibians, and small fish

GRAY-BANDED KINGSNAKE

(LAMPROPELTIS ALTERNA)

Gray-banded kingsnakes have gray bodies circled by reddish-orange bands. The thickness of the bands varies within the species. These nocturnal snakes are rarely seen. They hide underground or in rocky crevices during the day to escape the desert heat. They can hunt underground. Gray-banded kingsnakes may corner prey such as rodents in burrows. They also eat rattlesnakes. They are immune to the venom of rattlesnakes in their region.

FUN FACT

The word *king* in a snake's common name indicates that the snake eats other snakes.

HOW TO SPOT

Length: 3 to 4 feet (0.9 to 1.2 m)

North American Range: Southern New Mexico, southwestern Texas, and northern Mexico

Habitat: Rocky deserts and mountains

Diet: Lizards, frogs, rodents, bird eggs, and other snakes

KIRTLAND'S SNAKE

(CLONOPHIS KIRTLANDII)

The top of the Kirtland's snake appears dull in color. It is mostly brown or rusty red. Dark splotches cover its body. It has a black head. The snake is easily recognized by its belly, which is red. Small black spots border the red stripe on its underside. Kirtland's snakes spend much of their time underground. They overwinter in crayfish burrows. They also shelter underground during hot weather. Kirtland's snakes are rare throughout their range. They are endangered due to habitat destruction. The snakes make their home in prairies and grasslands. Much of this habitat has been destroyed for human development.

HOW TO SPOT

Length: 1.2 to 1.5 feet (0.4 to 0.5 m)

North American Range: Midwestern United States

Habitat: Open meadows and wet prairies

Diet: Earthworms, slugs, crayfish, leeches, small fish, and insects

LINED SNAKE

(TROPIDOCLONION LINEATUM)

Lined snakes are striped snakes that are sometimes confused with garter snakes. They tend to be similar colors, including gray, brown, and tan. Lined snakes also have three stripes running along their bodies. These stripes may be white, light gray, or yellow. The pattern of the belly is one of the main differences between lined snakes and garter snakes. Lined snakes have pale bellies with two rows of black, semicircle-shaped marks. Garter snakes lack these markings. Lined snakes shelter under logs and rocks during the day. They are more active at night, especially after rainfall, when they come out to hunt earthworms.

HOW TO SPOT

Length: 9 to 15 inches (23 to 38 cm)

North American Range: Central United States

Habitat: Grasslands and open woodlands

Diet: Earthworms, insects, and slugs

LONG-NOSED SNAKE

(RHINOCHEILUS LECONTEI)

Long-nosed snakes are colorful. Patterns vary across individuals. The snakes can have bands or splotches covering their bodies. They tend to have a mixture of white, yellow, and red markings. This coloration is similar to that of venomous coral snakes. But the bands of long-nosed snakes do not surround the body. Long-nosed snakes have cream undersides. They also have a longer nose compared to coral snakes. Long-nosed snakes are not venomous. They defend themselves in other ways. They shake their tails and thrash when threatened. They also release blood and feces from their cloaca as a defense method.

HOW TO SPOT

Length: 1.8 to 2.7 feet (0.5 to 0.8 m)

North American Range: Southwestern United States and Mexico

Habitat: Deserts, dry prairies, river valleys, and shrublands

Diet: Lizards, lizard eggs, other snakes, small mammals, and birds

WHAT IS A CLOACA?

The cloaca is a body part that all reptiles have. It is the opening that excretes feces, urine, and reproductive material. *Cloaca* is Latin for "sewer." Other animals also have cloacae, including amphibians, birds, and some groups of fish.

MEXICAN GARTER SNAKE

(THAMNOPHIS EQUES)

Mexican garter snakes are olive in color. A yellow stripe runs down the back as well as each side of the body. These stripes become darker as they approach the tail. A light-colored crescent mark is at the corners of the snake's mouth. Mexican garter snakes mate in the fall or early spring. Females can store sperm for later fertilization, usually in March or April. Garter snake species, including the Mexican garter snake, give birth to live young. Mexican garter snakes give birth to about 10 to 20 young per year.

HOW TO SPOT

Length: 1.5 to 3.3 feet (0.5 to 1 m)

North American Range: Arizona and Mexico

Habitat: Near water in deserts and grasslands

Diet: Frogs, tadpoles, fish, lizards, and mice

MILK SNAKE

(LAMPROPELTIS TRIANGULUM)

Milk snakes are gray or tan. They have red or brown splotches or rings with black borders. These nonvenomous snakes are similar in appearance to the venomous copperhead. But unlike the copperhead, milk snakes often have a pale Y-shaped or V-shaped mark on the back of the head. Milk snakes are nocturnal. They are solitary creatures that gather in groups only during hibernation.

HOW TO SPOT

Length: 1.2 to 5.8 feet (0.4 to 1.8 m)

North American Range: Southern Canada, eastern United States, Mexico, and Central America

Habitat: Woodlands, bogs, swamps, and marshes

Diet: Rodents, birds, lizards, snakes, and eggs

FUN FACT

Milk snakes got their name because they are often spotted near barns. People once thought they drank milk, but the snakes actually hunt rodents in these locations.

MISSISSIPPI GREEN WATER SNAKE *(NERODIA CYCLOPION)*

Mississippi green water snakes are dark green snakes with thick bodies. They have dark markings along their backs and sides. These markings tend to be more distinct in younger snakes. They fade as the snakes grow older. The snakes have gray bellies with light markings shaped like half-moons. Mississippi green water snakes have a small row of scales between their eyes and lips. This row of scales can help people differentiate the Mississippi green water snake from other water snake species.

HOW TO SPOT

Length: 2.5 to 3.8 feet (0.8 to 1.2 m)

North American Range: Central and southeastern United States

Habitat: Wetlands and swamps

Diet: Fish, amphibians, and crayfish

MOUNTAIN PATCHNOSE SNAKE

(SALVADORA GRAHAMIAE)

The mountain patchnose snake is named for the large triangular scale on the tip of its snout. It has smooth scales and two black stripes along its back. The region on its back between the stripes may be slightly more orange than its sides. The snake has a pale underbelly. It has large eyes and round pupils. The mountain patchnose snake lives in rocky areas at high elevations above 4,000 feet (1,220 m). It hibernates in rocky crevices. The snake slithers quickly. It is diurnal and spends most of its time on the ground, but it can also climb shrubs.

HOW TO SPOT

Length: 1.8 to 3.9 feet (0.5 to 1.2 m)

North American Range: Southwestern United States and northern Mexico

Habitat: Desert mountains and rocky woodlands

Diet: Lizards, snakes, small mammals, reptile eggs, and birds

MUD SNAKE *(FARANCIA ABACURA)*

Mud snakes are glossy, black snakes. Their scales shimmer in the sunlight, giving the snakes an iridescent blue appearance. Mud snakes are best identified by their bellies, which have a pattern of red and black bars. They have red eyes and yellow chins and throats. Mud snakes have a spine at the tip of their tails. This spine allows them to hold slippery prey in place and is also used for defense.

HOW TO SPOT

Length: 3.3 to 4.5 feet (1 to 1.4 m)

North American Range: Southeastern United States

Habitat: Swamps, marshes, bays, and slow-moving bodies of water

Diet: Large salamanders, frogs, and fish

FUN FACT

Female mud snakes stay with their eggs before they hatch. They leave the nesting site only to feed or shed their skin.

NIGHT SNAKE *(HYPSIGLENA TORQUATA)*

As its name suggests, the night snake is nocturnal. It hides in burrows and rocky crevices during the day. The night snake is pale with dark splotches extending down its body and has a white underbelly. It has a triangular head. The snake is similar in appearance to a young rattlesnake. However, the night snake does not have a rattle. It flattens its neck and hisses in defense. The night snake has a mild venom that helps it overpower its prey. In general, the venom is too weak to affect humans. But a subspecies in Texas has more potent venom that can harm people.

HOW TO SPOT

Length: 1 to 2.2 feet (0.3 to 0.7 m)

North American Range: Western Canada, western United States, and Mexico

Habitat: Rocky areas of grasslands, deserts, scrublands, and woodlands

Diet: Lizards, small snakes, frogs, salamanders, and mice

NORTHERN WATER SNAKE

(NERODIA SIPEDON)

The northern water snake has gray or tan scales. Dark bands cover its body. These bands are more visible when the snake is wet. Young snakes have brighter colors. The pattern fades as the snake ages, so older snakes may appear to be a single dark color. The northern water snake is active during the day. This snake is a strong swimmer. It hunts for aquatic prey and can stay underwater for about an hour. It is often seen basking on branches near the water.

FUN FACT

Saliva from the northern water snake has chemicals that prevent blood from clotting. Saliva from this snake is not harmful to humans.

HOW TO SPOT

Length: 2 to 3.5 feet (0.6 to 1.1 m)

North American Range: Southern Canada and eastern and central United States

Habitat: Near water

Diet: Fish and amphibians

NORTHWESTERN GARTER SNAKE *(THAMNOPHIS ORDINOIDES)*

Northwestern garter snakes are darkly colored. They have three stripes—one along the back and one on each side. Coloration varies across individuals. Their bodies may be black or brown. Their stripes may be white, yellow, turquoise, or blue. Some northwestern garter snakes have spots above the stripes on their sides. Northwestern garter snakes flee from danger. Escape behavior differs depending on the snake's scale pattern. Snakes with only stripes dart in a straight line before reversing directions. The movement the stripes make on their bodies confuses predators. Snakes with spots tend to slither away and freeze. The spots help them blend with their surroundings.

HOW TO SPOT

Length: 8.9 to 37 inches (23 to 94 cm)

North American Range: Southwestern Canada and northwestern United States

Habitat: Grasslands and forest edges

Diet: Slugs, earthworms, and small amphibians

PINE SNAKE *(PITUOPHIS MELANOLEUCUS)*

The pine snake is a large snake with dark splotches. The rest of its body is light brown or gray. Pine snakes have a pointed snout that is similar in shape to a turtle's snout. The snout helps the snake burrow underground, where it spends much of its time. Underground burrows help the snake escape daytime heat. They protect pine snakes from predators such as raccoons and foxes. Pine snakes hunt mice in burrows. These snakes kill using constriction. Pine snakes can imitate rattlesnakes. They coil up and hiss loudly. Their hiss sounds like a rattlesnake's rattle. Pine snakes also shake their tails in a similar way to a rattlesnake.

HOW TO SPOT

Length: 3 to 8.3 feet (0.9 to 2.5 m)

North American Range: Eastern United States

Habitat: Dry forests

Diet: Small mammals, birds, and bird eggs

PINE WOODS SNAKE

(RHADINAEA FLAVILATA)

Pine woods snakes range from orange to brown. Their scales have a reddish tint. They are thin snakes with white or yellow lips. Their bellies are a similar color to their lips. A dark line of scales runs through each eye to the corner of the mouth. Pine woods snakes are nocturnal. They hide during the day. They often shelter in rotting logs or under leaf litter. Pine woods snakes swallow small prey. They inject venom to help paralyze larger prey. This venom is too weak to pose a threat to humans. The snake is not known to bite people.

HOW TO SPOT

Length: 10 to 13 inches (25 to 33 cm)

North American Range: Southeastern United States, primarily Florida

Habitat: Pinelands, bayheads, and barrier islands with abundant leaf litter

Diet: Small lizards, snakes, amphibians, and earthworms

PLAIN-BELLIED WATER SNAKE

(NERODIA ERYTHROGASTER)

The plain-bellied water snake has a yellow underside. Its neck and lips are also yellow. Its belly is a solid color with no pattern. The rest of the snake is gray or brownish black. It has a thick body. The plain-bellied water snake lives near aquatic habitats, such as swamps. It basks on shores and on branches overhanging water. During very hot weather, the plain-bellied water snake moves upland to higher and drier areas to rest. The snake also hibernates in the uplands. The plain-bellied water snake is fairly active. It moves between wetlands several times throughout the year.

HOW TO SPOT

Length: 2.5 to 4 feet (0.8 to 1.2 m)

North American Range: Eastern United States and northeastern Mexico

Habitat: Near slow-moving water and swamps

Diet: Fish, amphibians, tadpoles, and crayfish

PLAINS BLACK-HEADED SNAKE

(TANTILLA NIGRICEPS)

The plains black-headed snake is tan with smooth scales. Its small head is shaped like a triangle. A dark patch of scales covers the top of its head and neck. The snake has a white belly. The plains black-headed snake is nocturnal, hiding under rocks during the day. It burrows deep underground during the winter. Scientists have found these snakes hibernating in burrows eight feet (2.4 m) belowground. The snake is active during warm months and breeds in the spring. Females lay a clutch, or nest of eggs, each year. Each clutch includes about one to four eggs.

HOW TO SPOT

Length: 7 to 15 inches (18 to 38 cm)

North American Range: South-central United States and Mexico

Habitat: Desert scrublands and grasslands

Diet: Centipedes, spiders, insects, and earthworms

PLAINS GARTER SNAKE

(THAMNOPHIS RADIX)

The main color of the plains garter snake is olive, brown, or greenish gray. Like other garter snake species, a series of three stripes runs along the snake's body. The stripe down its back is a bright orange or yellow. The stripe on each of its sides is paler and may be yellow, green, or blue. The plains garter snake relies on its sense of smell to survive. During mating season, males follow pheromones to find females. Plains garter snakes use their sense of smell to find prey. They also use smell to find underground burrows for hibernation.

FUN FACT

Female plains garter snakes usually give birth to 10 or 20 live young each year. But some have more than 60 young in a clutch.

HOW TO SPOT

Length: 1.3 to 2.3 feet (0.4 to 0.7 m)

North American Range: Southern Canada, central United States, and northeastern Mexico

Habitat: Wet prairies and open grasslands near water

Diet: Amphibians, tadpoles, small fish, and small rodents

PRAIRIE KINGSNAKE

(LAMPROPELTIS CALLIGASTER)

Prairie kingsnakes are medium-sized snakes with smooth scales. They have pale brown bodies with a pattern of reddish-brown splotches. Each splotch is rimmed with black scales. The splotch on the top of the head tends to be shaped like an arrowhead. These snakes do not have distinct necks. They are solitary and spend much of their time hiding in burrows or under logs and rocks. Prairie kingsnakes buzz their tails in leaf litter when threatened. They also twitch their heads and pretend to strike.

HOW TO SPOT

Length: 2.5 to 3.5 feet (0.8 to 1.1 m)

North American Range: Southeastern and central United States

Habitat: Prairies, farmlands, woodland edges, and rocky hillsides

Diet: Small mammals, lizards, and small snakes

PAYING ATTENTION TO PATTERNS

Prairie kingsnakes are often confused for copperheads, which are venomous. Both are brown with splotches. However, they have slightly different patterns. The splotches on prairie kingsnakes are rounded or saddle shaped. Copperheads have hourglass-shaped markings.

QUEEN SNAKE *(REGINA SEPTEMVITTATA)*

Queen snakes have rough scales that are gray or olive brown. Three dark stripes run along their backs. They also have a whitish-cream stripe on each side. Their bellies are cream with two brown stripes running down the length. Queen snakes often bask on low-hanging branches over slow-moving waters. If disturbed, they drop into the water. There, they take cover at the bottom or swim a short distance away. Most snakes that eat crayfish choose hard-shelled ones. But queen snakes eat mostly molting crayfish. It is easier for queen snakes to digest crayfish without the tough exoskeletons.

HOW TO SPOT

Length: 1.1 to 3 feet (0.3 to 0.9 m)

North American Range: Eastern United States

Habitat: Mountains and near rocky streams and small rivers

Diet: Molting crayfish

RAINBOW SNAKE

(FARANCIA ERYTROGRAMMA)

Rainbow snakes are named for their stunning appearance. This glossy black snake appears iridescent in direct sunlight. Three thin red stripes run down its back. Its underside, including the chin and throat, is yellow. A pointy scale at the tip of its tail helps the snake catch prey. A rainbow snake drags aquatic prey to the shore, where it swallows the prey whole. These snakes are nocturnal, spending much of their time hiding in aquatic vegetation or underground burrows. Rainbow snakes are rarely seen by humans because they are seldom on land.

FUN FACT

Because rainbow snakes eat mainly eels, they are also called eel moccasins.

Shedding skin

HOW TO SPOT

Length: 2.3 to 4 feet (0.7 to 1.2 m)

North American Range: Southeastern United States

Habitat: Large streams, small lakes, swamps, and marshes

Diet: Freshwater American eels

RED-BELLIED SNAKE

(STORERIA OCCIPITOMACULATA)

The red-bellied snake is a small snake with rough scales. It is named for its brightly colored belly, which can be red or orange. Most red-bellied snakes have dark bodies that range from reddish brown to tan to black. The base of the neck ranges in color from orange to yellow. This coloration may appear as three dots or a single band. A red-bellied snake generally has four faint stripes running down its back. Some have a single bold stripe down the center of the back. Other snakes may have both of these stripe patterns. The red-bellied snake flattens its body and releases a foul-smelling odor when threatened. It also curls its lips. The flexible lips help the snake grasp slimy prey such as slugs.

HOW TO SPOT

Length: 8 to 10 inches (20 to 25 cm)

North American Range: Eastern United States and southern Canada

Habitat: Moist woodlands

Diet: Slugs, earthworms, snails, and soft-bodied insects

RING-NECKED SNAKE

(DIADOPHIS PUNCTATUS)

Ring-necked snakes have a band of yellow or orange scales circling their necks. However, the ring may be incomplete on some snakes. The bodies of these snakes are darkly colored. Their bellies are yellow or orange and have black spots along the center. They flip over and expose their bellies when threatened. The bright color startles predators. These snakes also release musk. Ring-necked snakes are nocturnal. But they sometimes sun themselves on rocks during the day. They are not picky eaters, feeding on a variety of small prey. The snakes produce a mild toxin that is not harmful to humans. The toxin paralyzes prey.

HOW TO SPOT

Length: 8 to 14 inches (20 to 36 cm)

North American Range: Southern Canada, United States, and Mexico

Habitat: Meadows, prairies, and woodlands

Diet: Small lizards, snakes, amphibians, earthworms, slugs, and insects

ROUGH EARTH SNAKE

(VIRGINIA STRIATULA)

Rough earth snakes have rough brown scales. The snake's belly is light yellow or cream. It has a pointed snout. It may have a band of pale scales around its neck. This band is more apparent in juvenile snakes than adults. Rough earth snakes are occasionally seen in flower beds and suburban areas. They are generally solitary creatures. They spend much of their life underground or hiding under leaf litter and rotting logs. These habitats are home to earthworms, their favorite prey. The snakes grasp prey with their jaws and swallow living prey whole. Female rough earth snakes give birth to live young in late summer to early fall.

HOW TO SPOT

Length: 7 to 10 inches (18 to 25 cm)

North American Range: Southeastern and south-central United States

Habitat: Woodlands

Diet: Earthworms, slugs, snails, and insects

ROUGH GREEN SNAKE

(OPHEODRYS AESTIVUS)

Rough green snakes are slender with rough scales. The topside of the snake is green, and the underside is yellow or white. Rough green snakes are excellent climbers, spending much of their lives in trees. Their green scales provide camouflage in this habitat. These snakes do not bite, so hiding is their primary defense against predators. Their strong eyesight helps them hunt insects. Rough green snakes breed during the spring. Females lay about a dozen eggs during the summer.

FUN FACT

Rough green snakes turn blue shortly after they die.

HOW TO SPOT

Length: 1.8 to 2.7 feet (0.5 to 0.8 m)

North American Range: Southeastern and south-central United States and northern Mexico

Habitat: Forest edges near lakes and ponds

Diet: Insects and spiders

SALT MARSH SNAKE

(NERODIA CLARKII)

The salt marsh snake varies in color, ranging from gray to brown or slightly orange. The snake has stripes running along its body. In some snakes, these stripes may become splotchier toward the tail. The salt marsh snake is named after its habitat. It lives near salt water in marshes and estuaries, where rivers meet the ocean. Despite spending its life near salt water, the snake cannot drink salt water. Rain and prey provide hydration. A female salt marsh snake gives birth to three to nine live young. The birthing season is between July and October.

HOW TO SPOT

Length: 1.3 to 2.5 feet (0.4 to 0.8 m)

North American Range: Southeastern United States

Habitat: Coastal habitats, marshes, and estuaries

Diet: Small fish, small frogs, and fiddler crabs

SCARLET SNAKE

(CEMOPHORA COCCINEA)

The scarlet snake is a tricolored snake. It is not venomous. It has a thin, whitish-gray body. Red patches rimmed with black scales run down its back. It has a pointed snout, which helps it burrow underground. The scarlet snake is a nonaggressive snake that rarely bites in defense. Instead, it coils its body and hides its head. It may release a foul odor. The nocturnal snake spends much of its time underground or hiding under leaf litter. It is aboveground only at night. The scarlet snake has large rear teeth. These teeth puncture reptile eggs, making them easier to swallow.

HOW TO SPOT

Length: 1.2 to 1.7 feet (0.4 to 0.5 m)
North American Range: Southeastern United States
Habitat: Forests with sandy soil
Diet: Reptile eggs and small snakes and lizards

SHARP-TAILED SNAKE

(CONTIA TENUIS)

The sharp-tailed snake is reddish brown. It has red stripes along its body. Its belly has a pattern of black and cream bands. The snake is named for the sharp scale at the end of its tail. The tail likely helps the snake grip slippery prey such as slugs. The sharp-tailed snake also has curved teeth to help it position slugs while eating. This snake lives in moist habitats and prefers cooler temperatures than most other snakes. It is most active during the fall and winter. The sharp-tailed snake often shelters under logs and rocks. Several snakes may shelter together.

HOW TO SPOT

Length: 8 to 12 inches (20 to 30 cm)

North American Range: Southern Canada and western United States

Habitat: Woodlands and grasslands with moist soil, often near streams

Diet: Slugs, slug eggs, and salamanders

SHORT-TAILED SNAKE

(LAMPROPELTIS EXTENUATA)

The short-tailed snake is thin and gray. A pattern of black patches covers its body. Orange spots are found between the black patches on its back. The spots look like an orange stripe down the snake's spine. The short-tailed snake strikes attackers with its mouth closed. It makes a short hissing sound when threatened. It also vibrates its tail and jerks its head. The short-tailed snake is found only in Florida. It burrows in sandy soils and is rarely seen by humans. Climate change and urban development affect its limited habitat. As a result, the snake is listed as threatened under the Endangered Species Act.

HOW TO SPOT

Length: 1.2 to 1.7 feet (0.4 to 0.5 m)

North American Range: Central Florida

Habitat: Woodlands with sandy soil

Diet: Small snakes

SMOOTH EARTH SNAKE

(VIRGINIA VALERIAE)

The smooth earth snake has a similar appearance to the rough earth snake. However, the smooth earth snake has smooth scales. Its snout is rounded. The snake is gray, brown, or slightly red. Small black dots are scattered across its back. The belly is slightly paler than its sides. People seldom encounter smooth earth snakes. The snakes are nocturnal. They prefer habitats where they can burrow and find cover in leaf litter. Smooth earth snakes eat prey that are found underground, such as earthworms. Females give birth to live young between August and September.

HOW TO SPOT

Length: 7 to 10 inches (18 to 25 cm)

North American Range: Eastern and central United States

Habitat: Moist woodlands

Diet: Earthworms, slugs, and soft-bodied insects

SMOOTH GREEN SNAKE

(OPHEODRYS VERNALIS)

Smooth green snakes are bright green with smooth scales. They may appear more olive in color when they are about to molt. These snakes have white or yellow undersides. Smooth green snakes live farther north than rough green snakes. However, the range of the two species overlaps slightly. The two species differ in behavior. Smooth green snakes can climb trees but spend most of their time on the ground. Rough green snakes are often in trees. Smooth green snakes lay a clutch of 3 to 13 eggs each year. They lay the eggs in burrows other animals made.

HOW TO SPOT

Length: 1 to 1.7 feet (0.3 to 0.5 m)

North American Range: Southern Canada and northeastern and midwestern United States

Habitat: Moist grasslands

Diet: Small invertebrates and earthworms

A MATTER OF DEGREES

As with many reptiles, temperature determines the sex of smooth green snakes. Eggs that incubate at temperatures above 82 degrees Fahrenheit (28°C) produce females. Eggs that develop at cooler temperatures produce males. Climate change is causing average temperatures to rise worldwide. More female reptiles hatch as a result.

SONORAN MOUNTAIN KINGSNAKE

(LAMPROPELTIS PYROMELANA)

The Sonoran mountain kingsnake has red, black, and white bands along its body. The white bands are rimmed with black scales. The black bands are widest near the spine. They become thinner closer to the belly. The snake's nose is white. The Sonoran mountain kingsnake is similar in appearance to the venomous coral snake but is nonvenomous. Predators avoid eating it because of this similarity. The snake lives at high elevations. It is diurnal. The Sonoran mountain kingsnake kills its prey using constriction.

HOW TO SPOT

Length: 1.5 to 3.4 feet (0.5 to 1 m)

North American Range: Southwestern United States and northern Mexico

Habitat: Rocky areas and mountains near water

Diet: Lizards, lizard eggs, rodents, birds, and other snakes

SONORAN WHIPSNAKE

(MASTICOPHIS BILINEATUS)

Sonoran whipsnakes are long and slender. They are olive or bluish gray in color. The snake has a cream belly that becomes more yellow closer to the tail. The Sonoran whipsnake has a broad head and large eyes. It uses its eyesight and speed to hunt. It raises its head above vegetation to scan for prey such as lizards and birds. Once it spots prey, the snake surges forward and captures the animal with its jaws. Sonoran whipsnakes do not constrict their prey. They swallow it whole. These snakes can be aggressive and will bite if handled.

HOW TO SPOT

Length: 2 to 5 feet (0.6 to 1.5 m)

North American Range: Mexico and parts of New Mexico and Arizona

Habitat: Rocky canyons with dense vegetation

Diet: Lizards, birds, and frogs

SOUTHEASTERN CROWNED SNAKE *(TANTILLA CORONATA)*

The southeastern crowned snake is small and harmless to humans. Its body ranges from tan to reddish brown. The head is black. Its neck has two bands. Pale yellow scales mark the base of the head. This band is followed by a band of dark scales. The snake's belly is white or yellow. The southeastern crowned snake burrows underground. It is most active at night, spending much of the day hiding under rocks and logs. The snake normally breeds in the spring. Females lay one to three eggs underground each summer. The eggs hatch in the fall.

HOW TO SPOT

Length: 8 to 10 inches (20 to 25 cm)

North American Range: Southeastern United States

Habitat: Sandy woodlands

Diet: Centipedes, insect larvae, earthworms, spiders, termites, and snails

SOUTHERN HOGNOSE SNAKE

(HETERODON SIMUS)

The southern hognose snake is a thick-bodied snake with a sharply upturned snout. This snout helps the snake dig up frogs and toads that are burrowed underground. The snake's body can be gray, brown, slightly yellow, or orangish red. The top of the snake is covered in dark splotches. The snake's belly is white in color. The coloration of the belly separates this species from the eastern hognose snake, whose belly is darker than its tail. The southern hognose snake puts on a display when threatened. It flattens its head, inflates its body, and hisses. The snake also flips over and plays dead to deter predators from eating it.

Playing dead

HOW TO SPOT

Length: 1.5 to 1.8 feet (0.46 to 0.55 m)

North American Range: Southeastern United States

Habitat: Woodlands and fields with sandy soil

Diet: Frogs, toads, lizards, and small mammals

SOUTHERN WATER SNAKE

(NERODIA FASCIATA)

Southern water snakes are darkly colored snakes with thick bodies. They have thick, dark bands across their backs that alternate with thinner, lighter bands. As these snakes age, their pattern becomes less clear. Older adults may appear to be a uniform black color. A dark stripe extends from each eye to the jaw. Southern water snakes will strike if captured, but they are generally nonaggressive. They vibrate their tails in leaf litter and release musk when threatened. They rely on their speed and flee into the water to escape danger. Their dark coloring makes it difficult for predators to spot them when they are fully submerged.

HOW TO SPOT

Length: 1.8 to 3.5 feet (0.5 to 1.1 m)

North American Range: Southeastern United States

Habitat: Near shallow bodies of water such as swamps, ponds, and marshes

Diet: Frogs and fish

SPECKLED RACER

(DRYMOBIUS MARGARITIFERUS)

The unique scales of the speckled racer make it easy to identify. Each of the snake's scales has three colors. The inner edge is blue, the center is yellow, and the outer edge is black. The tricolored scales give the snake a speckled appearance. The speckled racer can appear to change color depending on the viewing angle. It can look black, yellow, or green. Speckled racers are fast-moving snakes. They rely on their speed to avoid danger and catch prey. The snakes also have good eyesight and a strong sense of smell. They live near water so they can hunt frogs.

HOW TO SPOT

Length: 3 to 4 feet (0.9 to 1.2 m)
North American Range: Southern Texas, Mexico, and Central America
Habitat: Brushlands and scrublands
Diet: Frogs and toads

SPOTTED LEAF-NOSED SNAKE

(PHYLLORHYNCHUS DECURTATUS)

The spotted leaf-nosed snake is named for the large scale on its snout. The scale is triangular and shaped like a shield. It looks like a leaf is folded over the snout. The specialized snout helps the snake burrow underground. The snake also uses its snout to dig up reptile eggs, its main food. The spotted leaf-nosed snake is pale tan with dark splotches along its body. It is nocturnal and spends much of its life underground. The snake comes aboveground during early summer, when temperatures are cool. It hibernates during late fall and throughout winter.

HOW TO SPOT

Length: 1 to 1.7 feet (0.3 to 0.5 m)

North American Range: Southwestern United States and northwestern Mexico

Habitat: Deserts

Diet: Reptile eggs and small lizards

STRIPED CRAYFISH SNAKE

(LIODYTES ALLENI)

The striped crayfish snake is glossy brown. Three dark stripes run down its back. Its belly is yellow and slightly lighter than its body. The snake has a small head and yellow lips. Its round eyes are large for its head. These snakes are rarely seen away from water. Slow-moving waters are home to hard-shelled crayfish, which are the snake's preferred prey. Striped crayfish snakes bask in the sunlight when temperatures are cool. They spend more time underwater during hot days. Like many snakes, striped crayfish snakes release musk when threatened. They also play dead by becoming rigid and opening their mouths.

HOW TO SPOT

Length: 1.1 to 1.7 feet (0.3 to 0.5 m)

North American Range: Florida and extreme south of Georgia

Habitat: Slow-moving waterways such as swamps and bogs

Diet: Crayfish, amphibians, glass shrimp, and dragonfly larvae

STRIPED WHIPSNAKE

(MASTICOPHIS TAENIATUS)

Striped whipsnakes are long. Their dark coloring can have an olive or bluish tint. The snakes have long necks and large eyes. These features allow them to use a unique hunting technique. The snake slithers across the ground with its head raised to see above low vegetation. Striped whipsnakes have strong eyesight to watch for prey and predators. These snakes can generate a sudden burst of speed. They chase after prey and pin it with their bodies. Instead of constricting their prey, they seize it and swallow it whole. These snakes are good climbers. At times, they hunt from trees. They also climb into branches to escape predators.

HOW TO SPOT

Length: 3 to 6 feet (0.9 to 1.8 m)

North American Range: Western United States and northern Mexico

Habitat: Grasslands, deserts, and woodlands at high elevations

Diet: Lizards, small mammals, and other snakes

TRANS-PECOS RAT SNAKE

(BOGERTOPHIS SUBOCULARIS)

The Trans-Pecos rat snake ranges from yellow to tan. Dark brown H-shaped markings line its back. The snake has large, round eyes. The Trans-Pecos rat snake is nocturnal. It is rarely seen in the wild except during breeding season, which runs from May to June. Females lay 3 to 11 eggs in late summer. It takes about three months for young to hatch. This is a relatively long incubation time for a snake. Because the snakes hatch during the winter, the young often shelter underground until temperatures warm.

HOW TO SPOT

Length: 2.6 to 4 feet (0.8 to 1.2 m)

North American Range: Texas and northern Mexico

Habitat: Deserts and rocky areas

Diet: Rodents, lizards, and birds

WESTERN FOX SNAKE

(PANTHEROPHIS RAMSPOTTI)

Western fox snakes are gray or tan. They have dark patches on their backs and sides. Their heads are generally yellow but can also be orange. Because of this coloration, the nonvenomous western fox snakes are sometimes confused with venomous copperheads. Copperheads have hourglass-shaped markings, but the patches on western fox snakes are rounded. Western fox snakes are a type of rat snake, meaning rodents such as mice and chipmunks make up a large part of their diet. The snakes use constriction to kill their prey. Western fox snakes are diurnal. They sun themselves in their wetland habitats.

HOW TO SPOT

Length: 2 to 4.5 feet (0.6 to 1.4 m)
North American Range: Western United States
Habitat: Marshes
Diet: Rodents, small birds, bird eggs, and frogs

WESTERN GROUND SNAKE

(SONORA SEMIANNULATA)

The western ground snake is a small snake with smooth scales. Individuals of this species vary in appearance. Some western ground snakes are patternless, appearing plain gray or brown in color. Other western ground snakes have dark bands on their bodies. These may extend from head to tail or be concentrated on the front half of the body. The snake's belly is white with dark markings under the tail. The snake shuts valves in its nostrils as it burrows. The valves prevent soil and debris from entering the snout. The snake plays dead when threatened. It rolls onto its back and opens its mouth. Its tongue hangs limply.

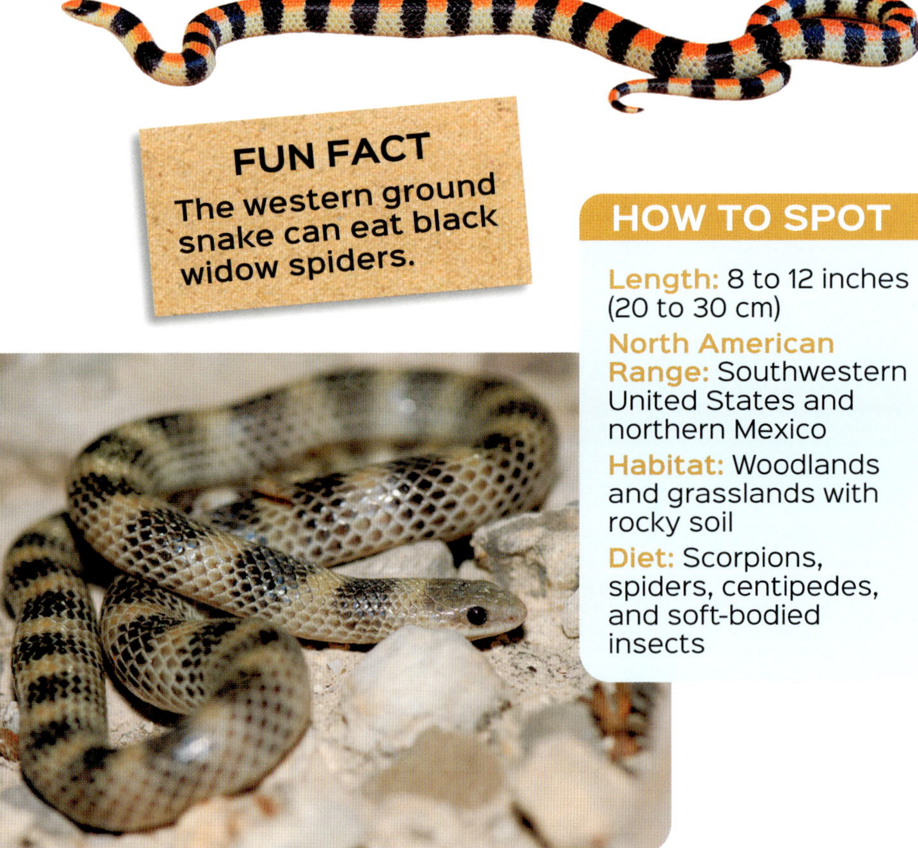

FUN FACT
The western ground snake can eat black widow spiders.

HOW TO SPOT

Length: 8 to 12 inches (20 to 30 cm)

North American Range: Southwestern United States and northern Mexico

Habitat: Woodlands and grasslands with rocky soil

Diet: Scorpions, spiders, centipedes, and soft-bodied insects

WESTERN HOOKNOSE SNAKE

(GYALOPION CANUM)

The western hooknose snake is a small snake that can be gray or tan. A pattern of brown bars covers its body, including a bar across its eyes that looks like a mask. The snake's snout is slightly upturned, which helps it turn over rocks to look for prey. Its belly is pale with a pink tint. The western hooknose snake is nocturnal and spends much of its time underground. It may come to the surface after rainfall. The snake has a unique defensive display. It jerks its body from side to side and is known to strike with a closed mouth. It pushes air out of its cloaca. This creates a popping sound from its rear.

HOW TO SPOT

Length: 7 to 11 inches (18 to 28 cm)

North American Range: Southwestern United States and northern Mexico

Habitat: Deserts

Diet: Spiders, centipedes, and scorpions

WESTERN LYRE SNAKE

(TRIMORPHODON BISCUTATUS)

The western lyre snake ranges from light brown to light gray. Dark saddle-shaped marks line its back. The snake has a broad head and a narrow neck. The western lyre snake is named for the V-shaped markings on its head. The markings look like a lyre, which is a musical instrument. The snake's belly is cream with brown spots. The western lyre snake kills small animals such as lizards with a weak venom. This snake kills larger prey, such as birds and small mammals, by constriction. Because of its defensive behavior, people may mistake the western lyre snake for a rattlesnake. It raises its body off the ground and shakes its tail.

HOW TO SPOT

Length: 1.5 to 3 feet (0.5 to 0.9 m)
North American Range: Southeastern Nevada, southwestern Utah, and western Mexico to Costa Rica
Habitat: Rocky canyons, hills, and mountain regions below 7,400 feet (2,256 m)
Diet: Lizards, birds, and bats

WESTERN PATCHNOSE SNAKE

(SALVADORA HEXALEPIS)

The western patchnose snake has an enlarged scale at the tip of its snout. This scale helps the snake burrow in sandy desert soils. It also helps the snake find prey, such as lizards and reptile eggs, that may be hidden underground. The western patchnose snake is slender with mostly tan or cream scales. Several dark stripes line the snake's body. A thick dark stripe runs down the center of its back. A thinner stripe marks each side of its body. The western patchnose snake moves quickly. It burrows underground but also comes to the surface. It occasionally climbs into low shrubs. The snake is diurnal and hibernates during winter.

HOW TO SPOT

Length: 1.3 to 3.3 feet (0.4 to 1 m)

North American Range: Southwestern United States and northwestern Mexico

Habitat: Lowland deserts with sandy soils and rocky areas, grasslands, and scrublands

Diet: Lizards, small mammals, small snakes, birds, reptile eggs, and amphibians

WESTERN RIBBON SNAKE

(THAMNOPHIS PROXIMUS)

Western ribbon snakes are thin with long tails. The orange stripe on the snake's back stands out against its dark body. A white stripe streaks down each side. This snake has a white spot on the top of its head. Its underside is pale and ranges from yellow to green. Western ribbon snakes are strong swimmers and flee into water to escape threats. Amphibians make up more than 80 percent of the snake's diet. This snake uses a unique hunting technique to capture frogs. It strikes three times with its mouth closed, startling the amphibians. When the frogs flee, the snake gives chase.

HOW TO SPOT

Length: 1 to 2 feet (0.3 to 0.6 m)

Range: United States, Mexico, and Central America

Habitat: Vegetation near bodies of water

Diet: Amphibians, fish, snails, eggs, crustaceans, and small mammals

FUN FACT

The western ribbon snake can shed its tail to help it escape predators. The unattached tail continues to wriggle to attract the predators' attention. The snake cannot regrow the tail.

WESTERN SHOVELNOSE SNAKE *(SONORA OCCIPITALIS)*

The western shovelnose snake is a small snake with a flattened snout. Its small lower jaw gives its head a shovel-shaped appearance. This head structure helps the snake burrow underground, where it spends much of its time. The western shovelnose snake has smooth, shiny scales. Its cream body is broken up by dark brown or black markings. These markings can look like bands that wrap around the entire body. They may also taper at the sides and be shaped like a saddle or an oval. Some individuals have orange saddle-shaped markings between the dark markings.

HOW TO SPOT

Length: 10 to 17 inches (25 to 43 cm)

North American Range: Southwestern United States and northwestern Mexico

Habitat: Deserts and scrublands

Diet: Insects, larvae, spiders, scorpions, and centipedes

WESTERN TERRESTRIAL GARTER SNAKE

(THAMNOPHIS ELEGANS)

Western terrestrial garter snakes are dark with rough scales. They usually have three cream stripes that run along their bodies. One runs across the back, and the other two are found on each side. However, these stripes may be faint or absent in some individuals. These garter snakes have gray bellies that are dark toward the midsection. Multiple males may mate with a single female, leading to a varied number of offspring. A female can give birth to as many as 19 young. They are born in the late summer or early fall.

HOW TO SPOT

Length: 1.5 to 3.6 feet (0.5 to 1.1 m)

North American Range: South-central Canada, west-central United States, and northern Mexico

Habitat: Near water in grasslands, deserts, mountains, and forests

Diet: Slugs, small mammals, salamanders, and lizards

WORM SNAKE *(CARPHOPHIS AMOENUS)*

At first glance, people might confuse the worm snake for a large earthworm. However, unlike earthworms, the worm snake has scales and small, black eyes. The worm snake has a dark brown or black back and a pinkish belly. It has a sharp scale at the end of its tail. Its pointed head helps it burrow underground. The snake digs through the soil in search of its preferred food, earthworms. The worm snake is harmless to humans. It is not known to bite. It squirms aggressively to avoid capture. When held, the worm snake may press its tail scale against a person's skin. However, the tail cannot break human skin.

HOW TO SPOT

Length: 7 to 15 inches (18 to 38 cm)

North American Range: Central and eastern United States

Habitat: Forests with rocky soil

Diet: Earthworms, slugs, and insect larvae

EASTERN CORAL SNAKE

(MICRURUS FULVIUS)

The eastern coral snake is a thin, tricolored snake. Its thick red-and-black bands are separated by thin yellow bands. The black snout is immediately followed by a yellow band that begins just behind the eyes. The eastern coral snake digs underground for prey such as lizards. It bites its prey repeatedly to inject its meal with venom. The snake's venom is toxic to humans. However, biting is usually done only if needed. The snake first tries to flee to safety. If this is not possible, the snake coils itself and ducks its head in the coils. It waves its tail in the air, causing predators to strike at its tail rather than its head.

HOW TO SPOT

Length: 1.7 to 2.5 feet (0.5 to 0.8 m)

North American Range: Eastern United States

Habitat: Woodlands and near swamps

Diet: Lizards and small snakes

SNAKE VENOM EFFECTS

Elapids and vipers produce different types of venom. Venom from elapids tends to affect the nervous system and cause paralysis. Venom from vipers targets the circulatory system and interferes with blood clotting. People should seek immediate medical treatment if bitten by a snake. They should administer basic first aid and clean the wound. It is a myth that venom can be sucked out of a wound. People should also avoid taking painkillers and should not put ice on a snake bite.

TEXAS CORAL SNAKE
(MICRURUS TENER)

Texas coral snakes are thin, tricolored snakes that look similar to eastern coral snakes. However, they have a different geographic range. The Texas coral snake has a rounded head. Red, yellow, and black bands encircle its entire body. The red and yellow bands touch. Texas coral snakes kill their prey with venom. Venom from the Texas coral snake is eight times stronger than venom from the diamondback rattlesnake. Encounters with the Texas coral snake are rare. These snakes are nocturnal and spend much of their time underground and under leaf litter.

HOW TO SPOT

Length: 2 to 3.3 feet (0.6 to 1 m)

North American Range: Texas, Louisiana, Arkansas, and northern Mexico

Habitat: Lowland areas and woodlands with soft soil

Diet: Other snakes and lizards

WESTERN CORAL SNAKE

(MICRUROIDES EURYXANTHUS)

The western coral snake is a venomous snake with a short snout. It has red, yellow, and black bands. The yellow bands border both sides of the red bands. The bands continue to the underside of the snake but are paler. The snake's head is black. The bright colors of the coral snake warn predators that it is venomous. The snake has other tactics to scare away predators. It coils itself and raises its tail. It pushes air through its cloaca, producing a popping sound that startles predators. The western coral snake spends much of its life burrowed underground or sheltering under rocks.

HOW TO SPOT

Length: 1.1 to 1.8 feet (0.3 to 0.5 m)

North American Range: Arizona, southwestern New Mexico, and northern Mexico

Habitat: Rocky deserts

Diet: Other snakes, also lizards

YELLOW-BELLIED SEA SNAKE

(HYDROPHIS PLATURUS)

The yellow-bellied sea snake lives in the ocean. The top of the snake is dark brown or black. Its belly is bright yellow. Some can be entirely yellow. The snake's nostrils are located at the top of the snout. This feature allows the snake to breathe when basking at the water's surface. The snake's belly is slightly pointed like the bottom of a boat. This helps the snake maneuver underwater. It uses its broad, flat tail like a paddle. It is an ambush predator that relies on stealth. It waits for fish to swim by and then strikes with its fangs. Its venom slowly paralyzes prey. Its venom is also dangerous to humans.

HOW TO SPOT

Length: 10 to 45 inches (25 to 114 cm)

North American Range: Pacific Ocean offshore of California, western Mexico, and western Central America

Habitat: Warm ocean

Diet: Fish and eels

FUN FACT

The yellow-bellied sea snake has the largest range of any snake species. It is found from the eastern coast of Africa to the western coast of Central America.

Tail

BAJA CALIFORNIA RATTLESNAKE *(CROTALUS ENYO)*

Baja California rattlesnakes are venomous snakes that vary in color. They range from tan to dark brown. Other individuals can appear grayer. Splotches cover these snakes from head to tail. The splotches on the head are somewhat rectangular, while the markings on the midsection are more hexagonal. A dark bar extends from the corner of each eye to the side of the head. Baja California rattlesnakes are social creatures that live together in small groups. These snakes hiss and rattle their tails to warn predators. They generally strike only prey and predators that are not scared of their rattle.

HOW TO SPOT

Length: 1.7 to 2.6 feet (0.5 to 0.8 m)

North American Range: Western Mexico

Habitat: Deserts, shrublands, and tropical woodlands

Diet: Small rodents, lizards, and centipedes

PIT VIPERS

Rattlesnakes belong to a group of vipers known as pit vipers. Many North American vipers, including copperheads and cottonmouths, also belong to this group. Pit vipers have pits between their eyes and nostrils. These organs sense heat. This feature helps the snakes locate prey, because living creatures give off heat.

BLACK-TAILED RATTLESNAKE

(CROTALUS MOLOSSUS)

The black-tailed rattlesnake is a thick-bodied snake with rough scales. It has a triangular head and a black tail that ends with a rattle. The snake's body is grayish or yellow and covered in irregular markings. Markings on its back may be diamond shaped with a yellow center. The black-tailed rattlesnake has silver eyes with vertical pupils. It looks like it is frowning because scales partially hang over its eyes. This rattlesnake is a sidewinder, meaning it moves sideways as it slithers. This method of movement allows the snake to move quickly across sand. The snake can also swim and climb trees.

HOW TO SPOT

Length: 2.3 to 4.1 feet (0.7 to 1.2 m)

North American Range: Southwestern United States and Mexico

Habitat: Grasslands, deserts, and mountains

Diet: Small mammals, birds, and lizards

FUN FACT

All rattlesnake species give birth to live young.

COPPERHEAD

(AGKISTRODON CONTORTRIX)

Copperheads are some of the most commonly encountered venomous snakes in the United States. They are named for their copper-colored heads, which have no markings. The rest of their bodies are copper, gray, or tan with dark brown hourglass-shaped markings. These markings are sometimes rimmed with white scales. The coloration helps camouflage these snakes in leaf litter. They lie motionless under leaves, logs, and rocks, so it is important to step carefully in habitats where these snakes live. Copperheads are social snakes that hibernate together during winter. They may also hibernate with other species such as timber rattlesnakes and rat snakes.

HOW TO SPOT

Length: 2 to 3 feet (0.6 to 0.9 m)

North American Range: Eastern and central United States

Habitat: Woodlands near water and swamps

Diet: Mice, voles, frogs, lizards, small birds, insects, and small snakes

COTTONMOUTH

(AGKISTRODON PISCIVORUS)

Cottonmouths are heavy-bodied, venomous snakes. They are semiaquatic and often found in or near water. They have dark bodies that may be olive, brown, or black. Dark bands can be on the sides of their bodies. However, these markings might not be visible on adults. Young cottonmouths are more brightly colored with copper bodies. The inside of a cottonmouth's mouth is white. When these snakes open their jaws as a warning, the white mouth startles predators. Cottonmouths also flatten their bodies to appear larger. These snakes wait for prey to come near before striking and injecting the animal with venom.

Young cottonmouth

FUN FACT

Young cottonmouths have yellow tails. They use their tails as lures, wriggling them to attract prey such as frogs and lizards.

HOW TO SPOT

Length: 2.5 to 4 feet (0.8 to 1.2 m)

North American Range: Southeastern United States

Habitat: Near slow-moving water, swamps, and canals

Diet: Rodents, frogs, fish, and other snakes

Flattened body

EASTERN DIAMONDBACK RATTLESNAKE

(CROTALUS ADAMANTEUS)

The eastern diamondback rattlesnake is the longest and heaviest venomous snake in North America. Its rough scales give the snake a dull appearance. It is mostly gray or greenish in color with black diamond-shaped markings across its back. A dark band of scales covers its eyes. Pale streaks border this band. The eastern diamondback rattlesnake can inject a large amount of venom at once. After striking prey, the snake waits for the animal to die before eating it. Without medical treatment, venom from this snake is deadly. But the rattlesnake attacks only if needed. It shakes its rattle as a warning and takes an S-shaped striking position.

HOW TO SPOT

Length: 2.8 to 6 feet (0.9 to 1.8 m)

North American Range: Southeastern United States

Habitat: Woodlands, marshes, and swamps

Diet: Small mammals and birds

Young diamondback

EASTERN MASSASAUGA

(SISTRURUS CATENATUS)

The eastern massasauga is a venomous snake that lives in the Great Lakes region. It has a grayish-brown body with dark splotches. Its belly is black without any markings. The snake has a triangular head. The eastern massasauga is a type of rattlesnake. However, it does not always sound its rattle in warning. It is more likely to remain motionless and rely on its coloration to blend in with its surroundings. The eastern massasauga hibernates in burrows during winter. People seldom see this snake because of its low numbers and solitary behavior.

Fang and venom

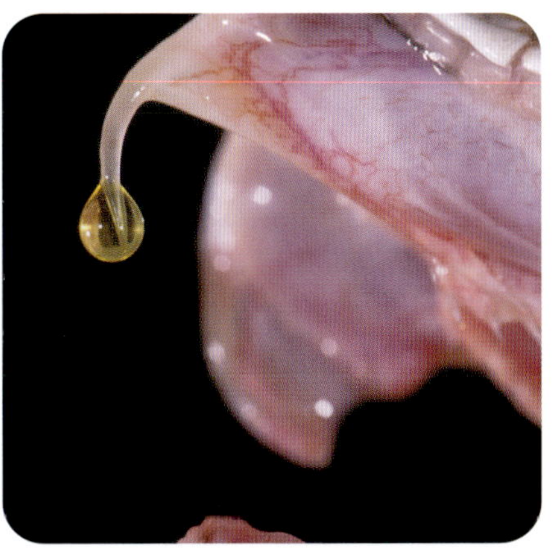

HOW TO SPOT

Length: 1.5 to 2.5 feet (0.5 to 0.8 m)

North American Range: Southern Ontario and northern midwestern United States

Habitat: Wetlands, fields, and woodlands

Diet: Small rodents, frogs, and other snakes

FUN FACT

The rattle from an eastern massasauga sounds like an insect buzz. It can be heard from about five feet (1.5 m) away.

MOJAVE RATTLESNAKE
(CROTALUS SCUTULATUS)

Mojave rattlesnakes are thick-bodied snakes with rough, greenish scales. They look similar to the western diamondback rattlesnake. Both species have a diamond pattern on their backs. However, the diamonds on Mojave rattlesnakes are slightly rounded. Mojave rattlesnakes have a thin neck and a large, triangular head. The venom from Mojave rattlesnakes is highly toxic. It affects the nervous system and also destroys blood cells. Medical treatment is necessary if bitten. However, bites from these snakes are rare. The rattlesnakes are nocturnal and not aggressive unless disturbed.

HOW TO SPOT

Length: 2 to 4.3 feet (0.6 to 1.3 m)

North American Range: Southwestern United States and north and central Mexico

Habitat: Grasslands, scrublands, and rocky areas

Diet: Small mammals, lizards, snakes, and toads

ANTIVENOM

Injecting antivenom is the primary way to treat venomous snake bites. Antivenom boosts the immune system. It has proteins called antibodies that counteract the venom. Antivenom is made by injecting tiny amounts of snake venom into an animal such as a goat or a horse. These animals begin to produce antibodies. Scientists extract these antibodies. They then purify the antibodies to make antivenom.

PRAIRIE RATTLESNAKE

(CROTALUS VIRIDIS)

The prairie rattlesnake is a large, thick-bodied snake. It is pale with dark patches on its body. These patches are ringed with white. White bands circle its body near the tail. The snake sheds its skin one to three times each year. Each time it sheds, the rattle on its tail gets longer. The prairie rattlesnake has poor vision. It tracks prey by sensing heat. It also has a strong sense of smell. This snake shifts its behavior depending on the temperature. It is usually active at dawn and dusk. During the hottest days of the summer, it is nocturnal. The snake hibernates in unused burrows during the winter. It returns to the same hibernation site each year.

HOW TO SPOT

Length: 3 to 4.2 feet (0.9 to 1.3 m)

North American Range: Southwestern Canada, central United States, and northwestern Mexico

Habitat: Grasslands and rocky areas

Diet: Rodents, birds, lizards, and other snakes

PYGMY RATTLESNAKE

(SISTRURUS MILIARIUS)

The pygmy rattlesnake is one of the smallest US rattlesnakes. It has a brownish-gray body with dark brown markings on its back. The markings range from rounded to rectangular. A narrow orange stripe runs from its head to its tail. The snake also has a dark stripe that runs from the corner of each eye to the jawline. The snake's rattle is small and produces a sound that can be heard from only about three feet (0.9 m) away. The pygmy rattlesnake sometimes follows scent trails to find prey. Defensive behavior varies across individuals. Some pygmy rattlesnakes remain motionless to avoid being detected. Others coil themselves, rattle their tails, and jerk their heads.

HOW TO SPOT

Length: 1.3 to 1.7 feet (0.4 to 0.5 m)

North American Range: Southeastern and south-central United States

Habitat: Near water in grasslands, woodlands, and marshes

Diet: Lizards, small snakes, mice, frogs, and insects

RED DIAMOND RATTLESNAKE

(CROTALUS RUBER)

The red diamond rattlesnake is a reddish-tan or reddish-brown snake with a thick body. The diamond pattern on its back is rimmed with white scales. Its belly is unmarked. Its tail has alternating black and white rings. Like other rattlesnakes, the red diamond rattlesnake has a wide, triangular head. This rattlesnake mates in the spring. Males compete with each other in a ritual known as a combat dance. They wrestle with one another. The stronger snake repeatedly slams the weaker snake to the ground. Female snakes have a long pregnancy for a snake, lasting around six months. Young snakes are fully independent. They have a grayer color than adult snakes.

HOW TO SPOT

Length: 2.5 to 5.4 feet (0.8 to 1.6 m)

North American Range: Southern California and northwestern Mexico

Habitat: Deserts, scrublands, and woodlands

Diet: Small mammals, lizards, snakes, and birds

RIDGENOSE RATTLESNAKE

(CROTALUS WILLARDI)

Ridgenose rattlesnakes can be gray, slightly brown, or orangish brown in color. This snake has pale bars with dark edges across its back. Its rusty coloration helps it hide in leaf litter. Some individuals have white lines on their faces. Ridgenose rattlesnakes are named for the upturned scales along their snout. Young snakes have a brightly colored tail, which they wiggle to attract prey. These snakes are diurnal. Ridgenose rattlesnakes spend most of their time on the ground, but they can climb tree trunks and rocky outcrops.

FUN FACT

All vipers, including the ridgenose rattlesnake, have retractable fangs connected to venom glands. Vipers can deliver dry bites, or bites without injecting any venom.

HOW TO SPOT

Length: 1 to 2 feet (0.3 to 0.6 m)

North American Range: Arizona

Habitat: Desert mountains

Diet: Lizards, mice, centipedes, birds, and scorpions

ROCK RATTLESNAKE

(CROTALUS LEPIDUS)

The rock rattlesnake is a venomous snake. It has dark bands on its light gray body. Males are larger than females. Young rock rattlesnakes have a yellow tail, while an adult tail is pinkish. The rock rattlesnake lives mainly on the ground. It can also climb into low vegetation. It often hides under rocks and within animal burrows. The snake hibernates during winter. It may hibernate alone or with other snakes, including snakes of a different species. The snake has a wider home range than other snake species in the region. It patrols an area of about 35 acres (14 ha) to hunt for prey.

HOW TO SPOT

Length: 1.9 to 2.3 feet (0.6 to 0.7 m)

North American Range: Southwestern United States and northern Mexico

Habitat: Deserts and dry grasslands

Diet: Lizards, invertebrates, small mammals, birds, and other snakes

SIDEWINDER *(CROTALUS CERASTES)*

Sidewinders are a type of rattlesnake that can be gray, cream, or light brown. Their coloration depends on their habitat. For example, sidewinders living in an area with light-colored sand are more likely to be cream. This color blends with the surroundings, so the snakes are more likely to survive. Sidewinders have raised scales above their eyes that look like horns. For that reason, sidewinders are also called horned rattlesnakes. Sidewinders are named for the way they move across the desert. Rather than slithering forward like most snakes, they wind their bodies and move sideways. This minimizes the contact their skin makes with the hot sand.

FUN FACT

Female sidewinders grow to be larger than male sidewinders.

HOW TO SPOT

Length: 1.4 to 2.8 feet (0.4 to 0.9 m)

North American Range: Southwestern United States and northwestern Mexico

Habitat: Sandy deserts

Diet: Lizards, small mammals, other snakes, and birds

SPECKLED RATTLESNAKE

(CROTALUS MITCHELLII)

A speckled rattlesnake's coloration matches its habitat. It can be cream or tan and often has a pinkish hue. It has irregular patches on its body that begin to look like bands near the tail. The speckled rattlesnake is diurnal for much of the year. In warm weather, it becomes more active at night. It hibernates during winter. The rattlesnake is an ambush predator, waiting for prey to pass near it. The snake strikes suddenly and injects the prey with venom. It uses its sense of smell to follow the dying prey. Like other rattlesnakes, newborn speckled rattlesnakes do not have a rattle. The rattle develops when rattlesnakes shed their skin.

HOW TO SPOT

Length: 1.9 to 4.3 feet (0.6 to 1.3 m)
North American Range: Southwestern United States and northwestern Mexico
Habitat: Deserts and scrublands
Diet: Rodents, lizards, and birds

TIGER RATTLESNAKE

(CROTALUS TIGRIS)

The tiger rattlesnake is a gray or brown snake with dark bars along its body. The sides of its body are orange or peach. The tiger rattlesnake is the only rattlesnake species that has bars near its head. It also has the smallest head of any rattlesnake. The size of its head helps it hunt prey. The prey may crawl into small crevices. The snake's small head can fit into these spaces. The snake injects venom into its prey and waits for the animal to die. Males and females of this species follow different breeding patterns. Males find mates each year following hibernation. Females mate every other year.

HOW TO SPOT

Length: 1.5 to 3 feet (0.5 to 0.9 m)

North American Range: Arizona and northern Mexico

Habitat: Rocky deserts and scrublands

Diet: Small mammals and lizards

FUN FACT

The tiger rattlesnake has the most toxic venom of all rattlesnakes. Bites generally occur only if the snake is being handled or threatened.

TIMBER RATTLESNAKE

(CROTALUS HORRIDUS)

Timber rattlesnakes are large, heavy-bodied snakes. They normally have pale bodies, but some individuals are very dark or almost black. The snakes have dark brown bands shaped like zigzags around their bodies. An orange stripe runs down the spine. Timber rattlesnakes mate in the late spring and early summer. They perform a courtship dance. A male timber rattlesnake slides next to a female. He rubs his head and body against her. Then he curls his tail under hers. After mating, males travel to habitats with more tree cover. Females stay in more open habitats.

FUN FACT

Timber rattlesnakes are skilled climbers. They have been spotted in tree branches more than 80 feet (24 m) in the air.

HOW TO SPOT

Length: 2.5 to 5 feet (0.8 to 1.5 m)

North American Range: Southern Canada and eastern United States

Habitat: Mountains, woodlands, swamps, and fields

Diet: Rodents, birds, lizards, and amphibians

TWIN-SPOTTED RATTLESNAKE

(CROTALUS PRICEI)

Twin-spotted rattlesnakes have gray bodies and orange tails. They are named for the two rows of small dark spots running down their backs. Like other rattlesnakes, twin-spotted rattlesnakes have a triangular head and slit-like pupils. A dark streak extends from the corner of each eye to the top of the neck. These snakes have a limited range and are found on only a few isolated mountaintops in Arizona and Mexico. They usually live in rocky areas where they can bask in the sun. They take cover under rocks when threatened. Twin-spotted rattlesnakes are diurnal and hibernate during the winter. But they sometimes come out at night and on warm winter days.

HOW TO SPOT

Length: 1.7 to 2 feet (0.5 to 0.6 m)
North American Range: Arizona and northern Mexico
Habitat: High-elevation forests with rocky soil
Diet: Lizards, rodents, and birds

WESTERN DIAMONDBACK RATTLESNAKE *(CROTALUS ATROX)*

The western diamondback rattlesnake is a thick-bodied snake with a triangular head. It has a gray body. It is named for the distinctive diamond pattern that runs along its back. The dark diamonds are outlined with white. Above the rattle, its tail is ringed with alternating black and white bands. The western diamondback rattlesnake is aggressive. It is one of the deadliest snake species in North America. It rattles and flattens its tail in warning. It also raises the front of its body into an S shape when threatened.

FUN FACT

The western diamondback rattlesnake can shake its tail back and forth 60 times per second.

HOW TO SPOT

Length: 3 to 5 feet (0.9 to 1.5 m)

North American Range: Southwestern United States and north and central Mexico

Habitat: Rocky areas and scrublands

Diet: Rodents, birds, and lizards

GLOSSARY

adapted
Adjusted to certain conditions.

aggressive
Marked by self-assertiveness or a readiness to attack.

bask
To lie in the warmth of the sun.

carrion
The flesh of dead animals.

constriction
The action of squeezing or making something narrower via pressure.

DNA
Deoxyribonucleic acid, which holds the genetic information of a life-form.

endangered
In danger of extinction.

exoskeleton
The hard external covering of certain types of animals.

genetic
Relating to genes, the information that influences development and physical characteristics.

hibernate
To spend the winter in a resting state.

iridescent
Having a rainbow-like or shiny appearance.

larva
The worm-like form of a developing insect.

molt
To shed an outer layer in order to grow.

musk
A strong-smelling odor.

paralyze
To cause to be unable to move.

pheromone
A chemical signal that allows animals of the same species to communicate with one another.

potent
Chemically powerful.

secrete
To form and give off.

semiarid
Having only light rainfall.

TO LEARN MORE

FURTHER READINGS

Eason, Katherine. *Big Snakes and Their Food Chains*. Cheriton Children's, 2023.

Murray, Julie. *Fun Facts About Snakes*. Abdo, 2022.

Somaweera, Ruchira. *The Ultimate Book of Reptiles*. National Geographic, 2023.

ONLINE RESOURCES

To learn more about North American snakes, please visit **abdobooklinks.com** or scan this QR code. These links are routinely monitored and updated to provide the most current information available.

PHOTO CREDITS

Cover Photos: Shutterstock Images, front (top left green, top right orange, top left peach, top center, top right brown, middle black yellow red, middle left blue spots, middle center orange and black, middle left light blue, bottom left, bottom center, bottom right), back (yellow, red) Interior Photos: Shutterstock Images, 1 (top left), 1 (middle left), 1 (bottom), 4 (top), 5 (top left), 5 (top middle), 5 (bottom right), 11 (top), 13 (bottom), 17 (top), 19 (bottom), 20 (bottom), 22 (bottom), 26 (top), 27 (bottom), 28 (top), 28 (bottom), 30 (bottom), 35 (top), 37 (top), 37 (bottom), 39 (top), 39 (bottom), 41 (bottom), 44, 47 (bottom), 48 (top), 49 (bottom), 50 (top), 51 (bottom), 57 (bottom), 58 (bottom), 59 (top), 59 (bottom), 64, 70 (bottom), 71 (bottom), 81 (top), 84 (top), 86 (top), 86 (bottom), 89 (top), 92 (top), 92 (bottom), 94 (top), 94 (bottom), 95 (bottom), 96 (top), 96 (bottom), 99 (bottom), 100 (top), 101 (bottom), 102 (left), 103 (top), 104 (top), 105 (bottom), 106, 107 (bottom), 112 (top); Matt Jeppson/Shutterstock Images, 1 (top right), 4 (bottom left), 4 (bottom right), 5 (top right), 7 (top), 7 (bottom), 11 (bottom), 13 (top), 16 (top), 16 (bottom), 19 (top), 25 (top), 25 (bottom), 34 (top), 40 (top), 40 (bottom), 42 (top), 42 (bottom), 54 (top), 54 (bottom), 65 (bottom), 67 (top), 73 (bottom), 76 (top), 78 (top), 80, 83, 100 (bottom), 101 (top); Eric Isselee/Shutterstock Images, 1 (middle right), 5 (middle), 21 (top), 107 (top); Natalie Jean/Shutterstock Images, 5 (bottom left), 10 (top); Tucker Heptinstall/Shutterstock Images, 6 (top), 24 (top); Brandy McKnight/Shutterstock Images, 6 (bottom), 24 (bottom); Larry Miller/Science Source, 8 (top); Wolfgang Kaehler/LightRocket/Getty Images, 8 (bottom); Suzanne L. Collins/Science Source, 9, 30 (top), 63 (top); Alexander Wong/Shutterstock Images, 10 (bottom), 88 (bottom), 104 (bottom); John Serrao/Science Source, 12 (top), 31, 93 (bottom); iStockphoto, 12 (bottom), 14, 63 (bottom); Susan Sheldon/Alamy, 15; Edvard Mizsei/Shutterstock Images, 17 (bottom); Michelle Gilders/imageBROKER/alimdi/Newscom, 18 (top), 66 (top); Danita Delimont/Shutterstock Images, 18 (bottom); Natalia Kuzmina/Shutterstock Images, 20 (top); Jay Ondreicka/Shutterstock Images, 21 (bottom), 45 (top), 49 (top), 58 (top), 60 (bottom), 61 (top), 61 (bottom), 62 (top), 66 (bottom), 98 (top); Jan Hejda/Shutterstock Images, 22 (top); Stephen B. Goodwin/Shutterstock Images, 23 (top); Steve Byland/Shutterstock Images, 23 (bottom); Daniel Heuclin/imageBROKER/Newscom,

26 (bottom); kristianbell/RooM/Getty Images, 27 (top); Steve Bower/Shutterstock Images, 29 (left), 29 (right); Marcus Rehrman/USGS, 32 (top), 32 (bottom); Nathan A. Shepard/Shutterstock Images, 33, 70 (top), 76 (bottom), 88 (top), 97 (bottom), 98 (bottom), 112 (bottom left); Jason Mintzer/Shutterstock Images, 34 (bottom), 102 (right); Tom Reichner/Shutterstock Images, 35 (bottom); John Sullivan/Alamy, 36 (top), 77; Brett Hondow/Shutterstock Images, 36 (bottom); Mike Wilhelm/Shutterstock Images, 38 (top), 38 (bottom), 51 (top), 55 (bottom), 57 (top), 65 (top), 85 (bottom); Photo by Paul Freed, 41 (top), 79 (top); Rusty Dodson/Shutterstock Images, 43 (top), 78 (bottom), 82 (top), 99 (top); Amy Surowiec/Moment/Getty Images, 43 (bottom); Patrick K. Campbell/Shutterstock Images, 45 (bottom), 50 (bottom), 55 (top); Stuart Wilson/Science Source, 46 (top); Viktor Loki/Shutterstock Images, 46 (bottom); Brian Lasenby/Shutterstock Images, 47 (top); Gerald A. DeBoer/Shutterstock Images, 48 (bottom), 53 (bottom); Andrew DuBois/Alamy, 52 (top), 74 (top), 74 (bottom); Jon G. Fuller/VWPics/Newscom, 52 (bottom); Joe Farah/Shutterstock Images, 53 (top); E. R. Degginger/Science Source, 56 (top); Charles Baker/Wikimedia Commons, 56 (bottom), 112 (bottom right); Melinda Fawver/Shutterstock Images, 60 (top), 85 (top); Kristian Bell/Moment/Getty Images, 62 (bottom); Anastasiia Pliekhova/Shutterstock Images, 67 (bottom); Oxford Scientific/Photodisc/Getty Images, 68; Todd W. Pierson, 69; Jeff Holcombe/Shutterstock Images, 71 (top); Paul Starosta/Stone/Getty Images, 72 (top); Klaus Mohr/Shutterstock Images, 72 (bottom); Khalid Alhadrami/Shutterstock Images, 73 (top); Randy Bjorklund/Shutterstock Images, 75 (top), 82 (bottom); Steve Schlager/Shutterstock Images, 75 (bottom); Bill Gorum/Alamy, 79 (bottom); Joe McDonald/Shutterstock Images, 81 (bottom), 91 (top), 91 (bottom), 95 (top), 105 (top); Ken Griffiths/Shutterstock Images, 84 (bottom); Matthijs Hollanders/www.flickr.com/mhollanders/Moment Open/Getty Images, 87; Jason Edwards/Photodisc/Getty Images, 89 (bottom); Jay Pierstorff/Shutterstock Images, 90 (top); Herpetology is Beautiful./Moment Open/Getty Images, 90 (bottom); Kristian Bell/Shutterstock Images, 93 (top); Chris Augliera/Shutterstock Images, 97 (top); McDonald Wildlife Photography Inc./Corbis/Getty Images, 103 (bottom)

ABDOBOOKS.COM
Published by Abdo Reference, a division of ABDO, PO Box 398166, Minneapolis, Minnesota 55439.

Printed in China.
052025
092025

Editor: Marie Pearson
Series Designer: Colleen McLaren
Production Designer: Ebonee Estrella

LIBRARY OF CONGRESS CONTROL NUMBER: 2024949009
PUBLISHER'S CATALOGING-IN-PUBLICATION DATA
Names: Lim, Angela, author.
Title: Snakes / by Angela Lim
Description: Minneapolis, Minnesota: Abdo Reference, 2026 | Series: North American field guides | Includes online resources and index.
Identifiers: ISBN 9781098297695 (lib. bdg.) | ISBN 9798384930211 (ebook)
Subjects: LCSH: Snakes--Juvenile literature. | Snakes--Behavior--Juvenile literature. | Reptiles--Juvenile literature. | Zoology--Juvenile literature. | Reference materials--Juvenile literature.
Classification: DDC 597.96--dc23